French Recipes

by Mary O. Hattery

Edited by Jeanne Wright

Penfield Books

The Author and Photographers

Some people cook so that they may eat; others eat because they like to cook. I am in that latter group. I have enjoyed compiling and adapting the recipes given here; they suit my tastes and abilities. I hope you will find them of interest and tasteful to your palate!

— *Mary O. Hattery*

Joan Liffring-Zug Bourret's photographs in this book were taken on a Seine barge trip in the company of friends, including Joan's spouse, Dwayne, and the Hatterys, Don and Mary. Cover color photographs by Joan include the Eiffel Tower, a market scene in Melun, and the back cover. Market scenes in black and white are by her unless otherwise credited. The inside colorful back cover and several market scene photographs taken at Tence are by Myrene Hoover, an art teacher for many years. Associated editors include Miriam Canter, Dorothy Crum, Melinda Bradnan, Dwayne Bourret, Peter Lucke, and David Wright. Graphics by M.A. Cook Design.

ISBN 1-932043-47-0 © 2008 Penfield Books

The Eiffel Tower

Alexandre Gustav Eiffel (1832–1923), an engineer and contractor, was known for wrought-iron lattices in bridge construction. He was awarded a contract to design the 985-foot tower for the Paris Exposition of 1889. Created from exposed iron, the tower was initially controversial, but became a world-famous symbol of Paris. Illuminated at night, the tower is beautifully reflected in the river Seine. The front cover view of the tower was taken from the deck of the Anacoluthe barge in the middle of the Seine.

The Fleurs-de-lis

Based on the iris, this design was used in the French coat of arms in the sixteenth century. The original French banner featured many fleurs-de-lis. The back cover of this book shows the fleur-de-lis in a castle window in France.

The Essentials of French Cooking

There are no new recipes. Here in our "melting pot" nation our palates are tempted by many culinary cultures, but none more so than the French. As Catherine di Medici carried her recipes from Florence to Paris (in Renaissance times), Julia Child brought her French recipes to America after World War II. Here we have an abundance of food and the means to transport it to the most remote hamlet. Technology has brought new processes and procedures. Ordinary cooks may bring the same food to their tables as French chefs offer at our topnotch restaurants.

The provinces of France, covering more than 30 regions, have distinctive styles of cooking and eating according to specific geography.

There is much respect for the pleasures of the table. Menus follow a seasonal pattern. Care is given to balance, variety of food, and tastes. The French shop daily and avail themselves of the freshest local food. The preferred custom is to gather the family together for the main meal in the middle of the day.

Classic French kitchens rely upon good wine and a variety of sauces to add flavor variation to a meal. Vegetables are often blanched to hold flavor and color and then reheated at serving time. Enrichment with *crème fraîche* is a common technique.

The French are remarkably slim and free from heart disease. They eat balanced meals with lots of vegetables and fruit, small portions of meat, and no snacks between meals. The preferred oil is virgin olive oil; fish is available in abundance.

The foundations of traditional French cooking are stocks, sauces, and aspics.

Basic stocks: brown, white, and, *court bouillon*

Basic sauces: *espagnole, velouté, béchamel*, tomato, *hollandaise*

Aspics are made by using commercial gelatin or making reductions of fruit or cooking juices.

It is important to understand that the set standards of French cooking are followed universally. Variations occur as similar methods are used and adapted to the food available in a particular region. With modern preservation and transportation, the specialties of a particular region are maintained and made more widely available.

There is a regional pride in a distinct food culture using local food — how dull it would be otherwise! Knowing the connection between the food you eat and the place where it is grown results in a universal comfortable feeling of "eating well."

By law, the French have established standards and guidelines for the production of certain traditional products. The superior designation, *Appelation d'origine contrôlée* (AOC), is given to wines and food products of great quality and individuality that are produced by traditional methods. *Confréries* or lodges are established to preserve and maintain the quality of valued food products.

Useful Terms

Béchamel sauce — made by stirring hot milk into a mixture of flour and butter.

Braising — a method of cooking meat that requires marinating, drying, and browning in heated oil. The meat is then put into a pan just large enough to hold it. Liquid is added, the pot is tightly covered to encourage self basting, and then put into the oven.

Canapés — tasty tidbits served on buttered toast.

Chiffonade — chopped strands of sorrel and/or young lettuce, to garnish soup.

Court Bouillon — a flavored vegetable stock prepared in advance for cooking fish.

Espagnole sauce — made by frying bacon and vegetables together, stirring in flour and brown meat stock.

Fines herbes — chervil, tarragon, chives, parsley.

Fleur de sel — "flower of the salt;" as in the top of the evaporating beds.

Foie gras — large livers from specially fed geese; primarily used in the preparation of cold terrines.

Herbes de Provence — fennel, rosemary, sage, savory, thyme.

Hollandaise sauce — made with egg yolk and butter, flavored with lemon.

Marc — spirits distilled with the residue of grapes after pressing for wine.

Mirepoix — finely diced vegetables cooked in oil and finished with Madeira.

Mise en place — elementary cooking preparations made in advance to be available for use at a moment's notice.

Roux — a thickening element made by adding flour to hot oil and cooking a short time.

Sel gris de Guérande — "fruit of the ocean, the sun and the wind," is another special seasoning found in Brittany.

Tomato sauce — made by frying bacon, carrot, onion, and garlic together stirring in tomatoes

Truffles — highly esteemed fungi that grow underground in certain parts of France. They are usually served sliced and raw.

Velouté sauce — made with butter, flour, and white stock.

Hors d'oeuvres

Hors d'oeuvres are meant to be the overture to the meal: to refresh and amuse the palate. They are best eaten calmly, with pleasure and anticipation.

Traditionally, the French like to have their *hors d'oeuvres* or appetizers at the table as a beginning course.

Arch, detail of the Eiffel Tower

Bettes au gratin — Swiss Chard Gratin

*Ruby red chard is especially good in this dish, but you
could substitute spinach as well.*

Preheat oven to 350°; spray 6 ramekins with oil.

1-1/2 tablespoons cornstarch
1-1/2 cups milk
2 teaspoons ground cloves
1 bay leaf
Salt and white pepper

3/4 cup shredded Gruyère cheese
3/4 cup dry bread crumbs
1/3 cup grated Parmesan cheese
1/2 teaspoon butter
3 bunches Swiss chard

Whisk together the first 5 ingredients; microwave 30 seconds, stir and repeat until thickened. Stir in the Gruyère. Combine the bread crumbs and Parmesan. Cut out the triangular core from each leaf of chard. Wash and coarsely slice the leaves crosswise. Heat a large pot of water to boiling and blanch the chard for 2 minutes or until wilted. Drain well; cool slightly and squeeze out excess moisture. Add butter and season with salt and pepper.

Mix the sauce and chard and divide among the ramekins. Sprinkle with crumb mixture. Place the ramekins on a baking sheet. Bake for 25 minutes or until gratins are set and tops are browned. Serves 6.

Tapenade

I first learned about this while on a cooking school tour in Provence; it has become a favorite.

1 cup pitted black olives
1/2 cup drained capers
3 anchovy fillets
1 clove garlic, chopped

4 tablespoons olive oil
Ground black pepper to taste
1 teaspoon cognac

Put first 4 ingredients into a blender and purée to a coarse paste. Add the olive oil 1 teaspoon at a time. Stir in the pepper and cognac.

Put into a ceramic or glass bowl; cover. Let rest for 2 hours or store in the refrigerator for up to a week.

Serve this on thin slices of baguette bread that you have toasted and stored in the freezer.

Olives are cured. If a white film has formed on your supply, rinse in water and store with a dash of salt, with vinegar and oil to cover.

D.H.

Terrine de coq — Chicken Liver Pâté

*To make this particularly tasty, use French Calvados brandy,
a specialty of Normandy.*

3/4 cup chopped onion
1 clove garlic, chopped
1/2 cup olive oil
1 pound chicken livers, trimmed
1/4 cup brandy

1/4 teaspoon allspice
1/2 teaspoon nutmeg
Salt and pepper
1/2 cup golden raisins

Sauté onion and garlic in oil until softened; add chicken livers and continue cooking until cooked through. Drain off excess oil. Add brandy and simmer

Detail of the Eiffel Tower

2 minutes. Transfer to a blender. Add seasonings and purée until smooth. Let cool.

Cover raisins with boiling water; let soak for 5 minutes. Dry raisins with a paper towel and stir into pâté.

Pack mixture into a crock and cover. Chill at least 6 hours or up to 3 days. Bring to room temperature to serve with crackers or toast.

Oeufs anchois — Stuffed Eggs

1 dozen hard cooked eggs,
   peeled and halved
1/2 cup sour cream
1/2 teaspoon Worcestershire sauce
1/2 teaspoon onion powder

1/2 teaspoon anchovy paste
1/2 teaspoon celery salt
1/4 teaspoon garlic salt

Remove yolks from white shells, mash, and add remaining ingredients. Stuff shells and refrigerate until serving.   Makes 24 servings.

Chèvre d'herbes — Herb-marinated Goat Cheese

10 fresh goat cheese disks
  (1/2-ounce each)
1 tablespoon chopped garlic
4 sprigs each of thyme, rosemary,
  and parsley

1 tablespoon chopped chives
2 tablespoons olive oil
Black pepper, coarsely ground
Honey, to serve

Place cheese in a single layer in a shallow dish. Sprinkle with garlic and herbs and pour oil over. Top with pepper. Cover and refrigerate up to 2 days. To serve, drizzle with honey and add toast rounds. Serves 10.

If you prefer a savory taste, use a flavored oil rather than the honey.

Coquilles Saint-Jacques — Sea Scallops & Mushrooms in Sauce

This is a very rich and very delicious treat!

1-1/4 cups dry white wine
1 cup water
1 small onion, diced
1/2 bay leaf
1/2 teaspoon salt
1/4 teaspoon black pepper
1 pound sea scallops cut into
   3/4-inch pieces

1/2 pound small mushrooms, thinly
   sliced
6 tablespoons butter
1/2 cup heavy cream
1 egg yolk
1 tablespoon flour
1/4 cup dry bread crumbs
1/4 cup grated Parmesan cheese

Simmer first 6 ingredients in a heavy sauce pan for 5 minutes. Add scallops and continue simmering for 2 to 3 minutes. Remove scallops and cool. Continue simmering liquid until is reduced to 1 cup, then sieve into a bowl. Cook mushrooms in 2 tablespoons butter for about 5 minutes; season with salt and pepper. Set aside. Melt 2 tablespoons butter, add flour and whisk for 2 minutes; slowly whisk in reduced cooking liquid. Simmer, still whisking for 2 to 3 minutes. Remove from heat. Whisk together cream and egg yolk. Slowly pour sauce into this mixture, continuing to whisk. Return to heat and simmer 1 minute. Remove from heat and stir in scallops and mushrooms. Season with salt and pepper.

Divide mixture among 8 greased ramekins. Top with crumbs and cheese. Broil until golden. Serves 8.

Croûtes de bouchées feuilletées — Camembert Walnut Puffs

This is easier than you think! These are the flavors of Normandy, however, Wisconsin Camembert is good, too.

1/4 cup walnuts, finely chopped
2 teaspoons butter, melted
1/8 teaspoon salt
1 frozen puff pastry sheet, thawed

1 large egg with 1 tablespoon water, beaten
6 ounces Camembert, rind discarded
1/2 cup toasted and finely chopped walnuts

Preheat oven to 400°.

Stir together first 3 ingredients. Roll out pastry on a lightly floured board to a 14 x 12-inch rectangle. Using a round cookie cutter, cut out 40 rounds. Brush tops of rounds with egg wash, sprinkle with walnut mixture, and transfer to a parchment covered baking sheet. Bake 10 to 15 minutes or until golden and puffed. Remove from oven; slide parchment off baking sheet to cool. While still warm, gently pull each round apart to make a top and a bottom.

With a fork, mash together cheese and nuts. Put a 1/2 teaspoon mound on each bottom and add top. Slide parchment back onto the baking sheet and return to oven for 2 to 3 minutes. Serve immediately.

Hunger is the best sauce in the world.
— Cervantes

Légumes au remoulade — Seasonal Vegetables with *Remoulade*

Any combination of vegetables may be used.
It is best to use those that are fresh at your local market.

Radishes   Asparagus
Green onions

Trim and clean the radishes and onions. Trim the asparagus. Set a large pot of water to boil. Add the asparagus, cooking it for 2 minutes. Remove the spears from the pot and immediately plunge them into cold water to preserve the bright color. Drain and set aside.

To make the *remoulade:*

1 cup mayonnaise
1 hard-boiled egg, finely chopped
1-1/2 tablespoons chopped
    cornichons or gherkins
1-1/2 teaspoons chopped capers

1 tablespoon chopped Italian parsley
    leaves
1-1/2 teaspoons chopped tarragon
    leaves
1/2 teaspoon chopped garlic
1 teaspoon prepared mustard

Stir together and place in a small bowl. On a platter, surround the sauce with
the vegetables.

Oignons — Broiled Onions

Spring "traveling" onions from the garden are especially good for this, otherwise, I use the small frozen variety.

3 cups baby white onions
1/2 cup beef broth

1/4 cup olive oil
Ground pepper

Simmer onions in beef broth until soft. Drain. Cut an "x" in the bottom of each onion and remove outer skin as necessary. Add olive oil and put onions into 6 greased ramekins placed on a baking sheet. Broil until nicely colored. Top with pepper.

Serves 6.

Tarte au fromage — Cheese Tart

1 to 1-1/2 cups all purpose flour
7 tablespoons of butter, chilled
   and cut into pieces

1/4 teaspoon salt
3 tablespoons ice water

Combine 1 cup flour, butter, and salt in a food processor. Process to coarse crumbs. Slowly add ice water, pulsing just until dough holds together. On a waxed paper, flatten the pastry into a disk, adding a little flour if sticky. Wrap and refrigerate at least 1 hour. Roll out on a lightly floured board. Using a 3-inch biscuit cutter, make rounds and place on a baking sheet. Chill for 20 minutes or up to 24 hours.

(continued)

Bake in a 375° oven for 20 to 30 minutes, watching for correct amount of browning. Cool.

For the topping:

1/2 cup grated cheese	1/4 teaspoon garlic powder
1/2 cup butter	1/4 teaspoon paprika

Blend cheese and butter until smooth. Add seasonings and spread on top of pastry circles. Freeze on a cookie sheet and then store until needed. Bake at 400° for 10 minutes or until lightly browned.   Serves 6.

For an easy variation of this, substitute three split English muffins or purchase prepared pie crust for the pastry rounds.

Grenouilles — Frog Legs

8 frog legs
1 egg beaten with
   1 tablespoon water
1/2 cup flour

2 tablespoons olive oil
2 tablespoons butter
1 clove garlic, chopped

Dip frog legs in egg wash and flour lightly. Heat oil and butter; add garlic. Sauté frog legs until crispy. Dust with minced parsley and serve with crusty bread.

Serves 4.

Gougères — Cheese Puffs

*An enjoyable drink with these tidbits consists of equal parts broth,
white wine, and tomato juice.*

1 cup water
1/4 cup unsalted butter
1 teaspoon salt
1-1/2 cups flour

5 eggs
1-1/2 cups grated Gruyère cheese
Salt and pepper to taste

Combine water, butter, and salt in a sauce pan. Bring to a boil, stirring until butter melts. Let cool slightly and slowly stir in flour. Mix well and return to heat. Stir in eggs one at a time until well combined. Add 1 cup of the cheese. Drop dough by rounded teaspoonfuls onto a greased cookie sheet. Smooth tops with the back of a wet spoon and sprinkle with remaining cheese. Bake at 375° for 25 minutes or until golden brown.

Serves 6.

French cooks often serve a cheese plate following the main course and prior to dessert. Up to four kinds may be offered, according to the number at table. The last of the meal's bread is eaten with the cheese. *Livarot, Comté, Cantel, Roblochon, Munster, Camembert* might be offered, along with local goat cheeses.

Market cheese

Cachet — Cheese Spread

Combine any hard cheeses, shredded, with 1/2 cup red wine and cream to cover. Pulse in blender until mixed. Let rest in the refrigerator for 24 hours or more. Bring to room temperature and serve with toast or crackers.

The French have access to many local cheeses; hard varieties are more readily available in the U.S. We have many excellent domestic cheddars and white cheeses that will work well in this recipe. Make this "ongoing" cheese spread by adding more cheese and liquids to the leftovers. This will keep for some time in your refrigerator.

Soups

Soup is to dinner what the porch
or gateway is to a building.
— Grimod de la Reynière

Pumpkin soup served in half a pumpkin in a Paris restaurant. Recipe page 47.

Beef Stock

4 pounds beef meat and bones,
  roughly chopped
2 large white onions
4 carrots, scraped
2 stalks celery

2 garlic cloves
2 whole sweet cloves
1 sprig of thyme
2 bay leaves

Brown the meat and bones in a 400° oven for 20 to 30 minutes, or until a dark color. Cut the vegetables into chunks. Tie the seasonings in a square of cheesecloth. Put all into a large pot with cold water to cover at least 1 inch. Keep at a slow simmer for 4 to 5 hours. Skim as needed. Do not cover. Strain the liquid off and discard the remains. Stock will keep in the refrigerator for 1 week or may be frozen for later use.

White Stock

1 (3 to 4-pound) stewing hen,
   cut into pieces
2 outer layers of a white onion
2 carrots, scraped
2 stalks celery

1/2 teaspoon whole allspice
1 bay leaf
1 sprig of rosemary
1 sprig of thyme

Cut the vegetables into chunks. Tie the seasonings into a square of cheesecloth. Put all into a large pot with cold water to cover by at least 1 inch. Keep at a slow simmer for 4 to 5 hours. Skim as needed. Do not cover. Strain the liquid off and discard the remains. Stock will keep in the refrigerator for 1 week or may be frozen for later use.

A supply of brown or white stock in the freezer is like money in the bank!

Soupe au cresson — Watercress Soup

3 cups thinly sliced leeks, including
    green part
4 cups peeled, thinly sliced potatoes
2 quarts water

1 cup watercress, packed
1 tablespoon salt
5 tablespoons cream
2 tablespoons butter

Simmer leeks and potatoes until almost tender; add watercress and continue simmering for 5 minutes. Pass mixture through a food processor. To serve, add either 5 tablespoons of cream or 2 tablespoons of butter. Top with parsley.

Serves 6.

If you are lucky and have some sorrel, substitute it for the watercress, for a sharp and tangy taste. To keep sorrel green, blend with butter and add toward the end of the cooking time.

Vichyssoise — Cold Potato Soup

This makes a great lunch on a hot summer day!

3 cups thinly sliced potatoes

3 cups thinly sliced white of leeks

1 cup cream

1-1/2 quarts of white stock

Salt to taste

Minced chives

Simmer until vegetables are tender; pass mixture through a food processor. Add cream. Chill. To serve, add salt and pepper to taste and top with minced chives.

Serves 6.

Soupe à l'oignon — Onion Soup

This is very fortifying on a cold winter day!

3 large sweet white onions, thinly sliced
2 cups dry white wine
2 tablespoons olive oil

6 cups hot white stock
6 slices French bread
3 cups grated Gruyère cheese

Preheat oven to 425°. Put onions, wine, and oil into a casserole. Cook in the oven until onions are soft and liquid is absorbed, about 40 minutes. Distribute the onions in 6 ovenproof bowls and pour stock over each. Top with a round of bread and grated cheese. Broil until cheese is melted. Serves 6.

Potage purée de pois cassés — Split Pea Soup

Green lentils may be used instead of peas; add a little tarragon in this case.

3 cups dried split peas, soaked
1 ham bone or 3 ham slices, cubed
2 quarts white stock
2 tablespoons chopped garlic
2 bay leaves

1 teaspoon dried thyme
1 teaspoon dried marjoram
2 onions, halved
4 whole cloves
Granish

In a large pot, cover the peas and bone with cold stock. Add herbs, garlic, and onion with a clove in each piece. Bring pot to a boil and reduce to simmer. Cook for 2 hours or until peas can be mashed with a fork. Put through a food processor. Garnish with a swirl of cream and a sprig of parsley or some slivers of sweet red pepper.

Serves 8.

Potage d'asperges vertes — Asparagus Soup

The potato thickens this soup just the right amount!

1-1/2 pounds asparagus
1/2 medium onion, diced
2 teaspoons olive oil

1 potato, peeled and cubed
5 cups white stock
Salt and ground pepper

Trim and clean asparagus spears, breaking off the tips, and cutting the tender stalks into 2-inch pieces. Bring a pot of water to boil. Add asparagus tips and cook for 30 seconds. Remove and plunge into cold water. Dry and set aside. In a large sauce pan, heat the oil and sweat the onions for 10 minutes. Stir in the

(continued)

potato and asparagus stalks. Add the stock and bring to a boil. Reduce heat and simmer for 20 minutes or until vegetables are tender. Let cool slightly and put through a food mill. To serve, heat through and divide among 4 bowls. Garnish with asparagus tips.

Serves 4.

Soup's enough, if there is enough soup.

*About 140 miles southwest of Paris is the **Loire Valley** with its vineyards, forests, gardens, and stately manor houses called* chateaux. *Many of the* chateaux *are open to the public, especially in the areas between the towns of Tours and Blois.*

Bouillabaisse — Fish Stew

3 pounds lean fish, such as halibut,
   snapper, grouper, sea bass, and perch
1 pound shrimp, peeled and deveined
1 pound fresh mussels
1/2 cup anise
2 tablespoons olive oil, divided
1 fennel bulb, trimmed, halved,
   and sliced crosswise
1 medium onion, sliced
1 leek, washed and sliced
1/4 cup chopped garlic, divided

1 quart clam juice
1-1/2 quarts water
6 tomatoes, chopped
4 new red potatoes, peeled and halved
3 sprigs thyme
4 pinches saffron
1 to 2-inch strip orange peel
Salt and fresh ground pepper
Fresh parsley
16 baguette slices, toasted

(continued)

Cut the fish into 2-inch chunks. Marinate fish and shrimp in 1/2 cup anise liqueur. Clean and wash mussels. Place in a pan and add cold water to cover by 1 inch. Bring to a boil and steam until mussels open; remove from heat. Remove mussel meat from shells and return to cooking liquid.

Warm oil in a large sauce pan; add onion, leeks, and fennel. Cook on medium heat until golden color. Add half the garlic; cook for 3 minutes. Add clam juice and water, vegetables, and seasonings. Cover and simmer for 10 minutes or until the vegetables are cooked, but still firm.

Use the potatoes from the stew for a *rouille*. In a blender, combine the potatoes, 2 tablespoons garlic, 2 drops Tabasco®, and 1/4 teaspoon cayenne pepper. Process until smooth. With the motor running, slowly add 1/2 cup of the stew liquid and 1 tablespoon oil. Correct seasoning.

Add the fish and the shrimp to the stew. Strain the liquid from the mussels and add to the stew. Simmer the stew for 8 to 10 minutes or until shrimp and fish are opaque. It is important to cook the seafood quickly.

Ladle the stew into shallow soup bowls, giving each an assortment of fish, shellfish and vegetables. Top with mussels and parsley. Pass the *rouille* to stir into the stew and/or spread on the toast. Serves 6 to 8.

It is worth the extra effort to make this traditional French dish.
A good soup must taste of the things of which it is made.

Soupe de alkekenge rhubarbe — Strawberry Rhubarb Soup

Serve this soup in white bowls to emphasize the beautiful color.

5 stalks of rhubarb, trimmed and cut
    into 2-inch pieces
1 teaspoon butter
2 cups hulled and sliced strawberries

1/2 cup orange juice
1/4 cup sugar
1 cup vanilla yogurt

Cook rhubarb in water to cover for about 7 minutes or until tender. Drain and cool. In a blender, combine rhubarb, butter, strawberries, juice, sugar, and 3/4 cup yogurt. Process until smooth. Chill for at least 1 hour. To serve, garnish with a dollop of remaining yogurt and mint leaves. Serves 4.

Potage purée de potiron au gras — Pumpkin Soup

For an elegant touch, cut a lid in a small pumpkin and bake until easily pierced with a knife. Cool. Remove lid and scrape out center. When ready to serve, reheat shell and soup separately.

1 tablespoon butter
1 tablespoon oil
1/2 cup chopped onion
2 medium apples, quartered, peeled, and diced
4 cups pumpkin purée or cubed winter squash
3 cups white stock

2 teaspoons ground ginger
1 teaspoon ground coriander
4 leaves fresh sage
Salt and pepper to taste
2 tablespoons maple syrup or honey
1 teaspoon nutmeg
1 cup cream
1/2 cup toasted pecans, chopped

(continued)

Cook onion in butter and oil until translucent. Add apples and pumpkin. Stir in broth and seasonings; heat to boiling. Reduce to simmer and cook until all are tender. Purée in batches in blender as needed. Stir in cream, sweetening, and correct seasoning. Reheat to serving temperature. Garnish with pecans. Serves 8.

To use fresh pumpkin or squash:
Lay a chunk of pumpkin on a flat micro-safe dish. Cover and cook for 10 minutes on high. Let cool and scrape flesh from outer skin. For a smoky flavor, stir in 1 tablespoon liquid smoke.

Market squash

Salads

Salade d'herbes — Herb Salad

1 teaspoon sherry vinegar
1 teaspoon red wine vinegar
1/4 teaspoon salt
1 tablespoon olive oil
Pepper to taste

1 cup mixed herb leaves: chives,
    parsley, dill, tarragon, mint,
    basil, oregano, and sage
2 cups torn lettuce leaves

In a salad bowl, whisk together vinegars and salt; add olive oil. Add mixed herbs, leaves only, pepper, and toss evenly to coat. At serving time add the lettuce and toss to mix. Use greens and herbs of the season. Serves 4.

With beef, parsley, dill, and chives are good. Fish is complemented by basil, dill, and tarragon. Use minced sage leaves for fowl.

Tomates à la provençal — Tomatoes as in Provence

6 medium sized tomatoes
6 anchovy fillets, rinsed and
    finely chopped
3 garlic cloves, minced
4 tablespoons minced green onions

1/2 cup minced parsley
1 cup bread crumbs
Salt and pepper to taste
3 tablespoons olive oil, divided

Heat oven to 350°. Cut the tops off the tomatoes, remove the seeds and pulp. Lightly salt the insides and place the tomatoes upside down on a rack to drain for 1/2 hour. Combine remaining ingredients using 1 tablespoon oil. Arrange tomatoes in a shallow dish and fill with bread mixture. Drizzle remaining oil on the tops. Bake for 30 minutes or until tops are lightly browned.   Serves 6.

Salade arugula — Arugula Salad

6 slices lean bacon
1 tablespoon lemon juice
Salt and pepper to taste
3 tablespoons olive oil

2 ounces Parmesan cheese
3 cups arugula, washed and dried
2 cups pitted black olives

Fry bacon and drain on paper towels. Break into small pieces. Whisk lemon juice, salt, pepper, and oil together in a salad bowl. Add the arugula to the dressing and toss together. Using a vegetable peeler, shave the cheese into strips. Transfer arugula to plates and top with cheese, bacon, and olives.

Serves 4.

Salade de lentilles — Lentil Salad

1-1/2 cups green lentils
6 cups white stock
1 clove garlic
1 teaspoon *herbes de Provence*
1 bay leaf
1 tomato, peeled, seeded, and
   chopped
3 green onions, chopped

1 tablespoon minced parsley
1 tablespoon capers
1/2 cup olive oil
2 tablespoons lemon juice
1 teaspoon Dijon mustard
1/2 teaspoon salt
Pepper to taste
1/2 cup goat cheese, crumbled

(continued)

Rinse the lentils and put into a sauce pan with stock, garlic, herbs, and bay leaf. Bring to a gentle simmer and cook uncovered until tender but not mushy, 20 to 30 minutes. Drain and let cool. Remove bay leaf and garlic clove. Put into a serving bowl with tomato, onions, parsley, and capers. Whisk together remaining ingredients, except cheese, to make a vinaigrette. Add to bowl and toss gently. Top with cheese. Serve with toasted French bread. Serves 6 to 8.

Nothing would be more tiresome than eating and drinking
if God had not made them a pleasure as well as a necessity.
— Voltaire

Salade de haricots verts — Green Bean Salad

1 pound young tender green beans
1 firm tomato
1 tablespoon wine vinegar
3 tablespoons olive oil

2 leaves sage, minced
1/4 teaspoon orange zest
2 shallots or green onions, minced
Salt and pepper to taste

Trim the beans and cut into 1-inch lengths. Peel, core, seed, and chop the tomato. Set in sieve, sprinkle with salt to drain. In a salad bowl, whisk together the vinegar, oil, sage, and zest. Bring a pot of salted water to boil, add beans and cook until just tender. Plunge beans into cold water and then drain. Wrap in toweling to dry. Add the beans and tomato to the salad bowl, stirring to combine. This may be served immediately and is also very good cold.   Serves 4.

Poires au cresson — Pears with Watercress

1 tablespoon lemon juice
2 tablespoons olive oil
1/4 teaspoon salt
1/2 teaspoon black pepper
2 firm pears, at room temperature

1/2 cup walnuts
2 cups watercress, cleaned and
    stemmed
1/2 cup blue cheese crumbs

Whisk the lemon juice, vinegar, oil, salt and pepper together in a bowl. Peel, core, and slice the pears into 16 slices. Add to the bowl and marinate for 30 minutes. Toast the walnuts in a little oil and drain on toweling. At serving time, add the watercress to the bowl and toss together. Transfer to serving plates and top with cheese and nuts.   Serves 4.

Salade niçoise — Salad as in Nice

This is a good main dish for a summer lunch, using any or all of the following ingredients you have on hand.

1 tablespoon wine vinegar
1 tablespoon lemon juice
1/8 teaspoon salt
1/2 cup basil leaves, minced
3 cloves garlic, minced
1/2 cup olive oil
4 potatoes, scrubbed, cut into
   1-inch pieces

4 cups lettuce, washed, dried, and
   torn into small pieces
1 green bell pepper, chopped
1 red bell pepper, chopped
3 celery ribs, diced
3 tomatoes, peeled and quartered
1 can anchovy fillets, drained
   and cut into small pieces

(continued)

3 cups green beans, cooked, drained, and dried

1 cup tuna chunks, dried

3 hard-boiled eggs, peeled and quartered

Minced fresh herbs

In a screw top jar, mix the first 5 ingredients; add the oil and shake well. Cook the potatoes until tender; drain and put them in a large shallow bowl. Add 2 tablespoons of dressing. Add the remaining ingredients in layers and top with remaining dressing. Serves 6.

French market lettuce

Salade de fruits frais au gingembre — Gingered Fresh Fruit Salad

6 plums, peeled, pitted, and sliced
3 peaches, peeled, pitted, and sliced
3 oranges, peeled, and sectioned
2 kiwi fruits, peeled, and sliced
1/2 small watermelon, peeled, seeded, and cut into cubes
1 cantaloupe, peeled, seeded, and cut into cubes

1 honeydew, peeled, seeded, and cut into cubes
1 pint fresh strawberries, hulled, and sliced
Juice of 1 lemon
1/2 cup honey
2 teaspoons grated fresh ginger
3/4 cup white wine

Combine the fruit in a large bowl; toss with lemon juice. Heat the honey and wine and stir in the ginger. Let sit for 3 to 5 minutes. Gently stir into fruit. Serve immediately or cover and chill.   Serves 10.

Salade colmarienne — Alsatian Sausage & Cheese Salad

*This is a popular winter salad from the Alsace area using the
local sausage, which is cervelas, and Gruyère cheese.*

4 shallots, cut into thin rings
2 tomatoes, peeled, cored, seeded,
  and chopped
1-1/4 cups minced chives
2 tablespoons wine vinegar

1/2 cup peanut oil
8 ounces precooked smoked
  pork sausages
8 ounces Gruyère cheese, chilled
4 cups curly endive, washed, and dried
Freshly-ground black pepper

Combine the first 5 ingredients in a screw top jar; shake to blend. Remove the casings from the sausages; cut into thick slices. Toss with 1/3 of the dressing. Cut the cheese into thin sticks; toss with 1/3 of the dressing and bring to room temperature. Cut the endive into small pieces and toss in remaining dressing.

At serving time, divide the endive among 4 plates. Top with circles of sausage and then cheese sticks. Season with pepper. Serves 6.

Eating is like making love. In France we put our whole bodies and minds into experiencing good food and wine. We savor both the food and the company.
— Chef Alain Sailhac

Vegetables

Asperges — Asparagus

The French method of cooking asparagus results in very green and tender spears. Peel the spears, if needed, and tie them in bundles and put them into a large kettle of rapidly boiling salted water. Boil slowly and drain quickly when tender.

8 quarts boiling water   6 bundles, each with 6 spears asparagus
2 tablespoons salt

Prepare the asparagus by peeling the spears with a small sharp knife from the butt to the bottom of the tip. Cut to make all the spears the same length. Tie together with string at top and bottom.

(continued)

Lay the bundles in the water and return to a slow boil. Cook for 10 minutes and then test for tenderness. When the spears bend a little, lift bundle from water and tip to drain. Lay on a dry cloth and continue removing bundles. Cut and remove strings and roll asparagus in the cloth to dry.

In preparation for cooking, you may prepare the bundles and hold them upright in 1/2 inch of water in the refrigerator until cooking time. Use a tall asparagus steamer for cooking if you have one.   Serves 6.

A traditional addition to hot asparagus is hollandaise sauce;
cold asparagus is good with a vinaigrette dressing.

Artichokes

Fonds d'Artichauts — Artichokes

Artichokes are good with chicken, veal, and egg dishes. This dish may be cooked in advance and reheated.

4 tablespoons butter
1/4 cup finely diced ham
6 cooked artichoke hearts
1/2 cup finely diced carrots, onions, and celery

2 tablespoons minced shallots or green onions
Salt and pepper
1/2 lemon

Melt the butter in a 6-cup casserole. Layer in the ham and vegetables; add salt and pepper to taste. Cover and bake at 325° for 15 to 20 minutes. Do not overcook. Squeeze lemon over all and serve.

Serves 6.

Petits pois frais à la française — Peas and Lettuce

This is a special treat in the early summer when garden fresh ingredients are available. For each cup of peas, buy 1 pound of peas in the hull. If there are peas left over (unlikely!), stir them into rice or pasta.

2 to 3 cups peas and shelled pods
Hot water to cover
2 green onions, thinly sliced

6 fronds of leaf lettuce, coarsely
    chopped
3 tablespoons butter

Put peas and 2 or 3 clean pods or flavor into a saucepan; add water and bring to a boil. Add onions and simmer 2 to 3 minutes until peas are tender, but not soft. Layer lettuce on top of peas. Let steam until water is absorbed by the peas. Drain and return to pan. Add butter, stirring until melted.   Serves 4.

Haricots verts — Green Beans

French green beans are about 1/4 inch in diameter. There are many other varieties of beans; the main thing is to buy beans that are clean, fresh looking, and firm. Snap the ends off and remove any strings. Leave the beans whole and all of equal length or cut into 2-1/2-inch lengths. Always give beans a preliminary blanching in a kettle of fast boiling water. This gives you good color and texture. They should be tender, but crunchy. One pound of green beans will serve 3 people.

Drop the beans into boiling water a handful at a time; simmer until tender, about five minutes. Drain immediately.

If you are serving the beans immediately, return to the kettle, toss with a knob of butter and season with salt and pepper and the juice of half of a lemon.

For later serving or to serve them cold, run cold water over the beans, drain, spread on a clean towel, and pat dry. Store, covered, in the refrigerator. To reheat, toss them in a skillet with butter or oil, letting them warm thoroughly; about 3 to 4 minutes.

It's so beautifully arranged on the plate —
you know someone's fingers have been all over it.
— Julia Child

L'oignon braisé — Golden Onions

Boiling onions may be used; parboil them for 2 minutes and slip the outside skins off before continuing as below. This dish may be served hot or cold; preparing ahead helps to marry the flavors.

2 pounds new onions, 2 to 3-inches
   in diameter
2 tablespoons butter
2 tablespoons olive oil
6 apricots and/or plums, quartered

2 tablespoons red wine vinegar
2 teaspoons honey
2 teaspoons finely chopped rosemary
Salt and pepper

Trim onions, leaving them whole and removing as little as possible. Heat oil and butter in a skillet. Add onions, stirring and turning them to coat. Continue cooking until onions start to brown; about 5 minutes. Add water to barely cover. Bring to a boil and simmer for 15 to 20 minutes until the onions have softened. Drain and add remaining ingredients. Continue cooking at low heat, stirring gently, until onions are a golden color. Serves 8.

A selection of famous French writers:
Abélard, Balzac, Baudelaire, Beckett, Camus, Colette, Diderot, Flaubert, Gide, Hugo, Ionesco, Molière, Montaigne, Proust, Rabelais, Racine, Rimbaud, Rostand, Rousseau, Sartre, Stendhal, Tocqueville, Verlaine, Voltaire, and Zola

Chou-fleur à tomate gratinée
Cauliflower with Cheese & Tomatoes

This is especially compatible with beef entrées.

1 (8-inch) head of cauliflower	Salt and pepper
1-1/2 cups diced tomatoes, drained	1/4 cup dry bread crumbs
1/2 cup melted butter	1/2 cup grated Swiss cheese

Choose cauliflower heads that are firm and white with compact flower clusters. Pull the leaves off and cut the clusters off the main stalk. Slit the larger stems so all will cook evenly. Blanch as in the green bean recipe. A steamer rack is useful.

When cauliflower is tender, remove rack and plunge into cold water, then drain.

Put cauliflower into the center of a shallow 10-inch buttered dish. Surround with tomatoes. Season all with half of the butter and salt and pepper. Top with cheese and crumbs mixed together and then remaining melted butter.

Bake in a 375° oven for 30 minutes or until nicely browned.   Serves 6.

The French Riviera (Côte d'Azur)
One of the most famous resort areas, the French Riviera stretches from the Italian border toward the west along the Mediterranean Sea, and includes the towns of Nice, Antibes, Cannes, and St. Tropez, among many others. Nearby is the area of Provence, with its hill towns and fields of lavender.

Tomates Concentrées — Dried Tomatoes

This is a great way to preserve summer's bountiful supply of tomatoes. These tomatoes may be a side dish, accompany the main entrée or used to bring up the flavor in a sauce or soup.

4 to 5 pounds firm tomatoes
1/2 cup olive oil

Fresh herbs
Chopped garlic
Zest of 1 orange

Skin tomatoes by dipping them in boiling water and then into cold water. Halve, then squeeze each half to drain juices and seeds. Place tomatoes on baking sheets covered with foil or parchment. Drizzle with oil and sprinkle with herbs, garlic, and orange zest. Bake in a 200° oven until soft and shrunken. Store tomatoes covered with olive oil in a glass container. Refrigerate until ready to use.

Pâtisson — Summer Squash

For best flavor, the squash should retain some crunchiness.

4 to 5 squash, peeled and cut into match-stick-sized pieces
1 tablespoon salt
2 tablespoons olive oil

2 tablespoons butter
1/4 cup chopped basil leaves
1/4 cup chopped chives
1/4 cup grated Parmesan

Toss squash and salt and put into a sieve over a bowl. Cover with a plate and a 2-pound weight and let stand for an hour. Dry with paper towels. Heat oil and butter in a skillet; add squash and toss together. Cook for 2 minutes, continuing tossing. Stir in herbs and cheese and serve.   Serves 6.

Endives à la flamande — Braised Belgian Endive

The process of a long cooking time results in a wonderful exchange of flavors. This dish may be cooled, covered, and reheated the next day. At that time, brush the top with melted butter and put briefly under a broiler.

12 medium-sized endives
6 tablespoons butter
1/4 teaspoon salt

1 tablespoon lemon juice
1/4 cup beef stock or broth

Trim the base of the endives, removing any bad leaves. Wash each under running water and pat dry. Spread butter in the bottom of a stove to oven pot and lay the endives in it to cover the bottom. Dot with butter and sprinkle with lemon juice. Continue with a second layer. Pour in the stock or broth, cover, and steam for 10 minutes or until the liquid is reduced to 3 tablespoons.

Lay a round of buttered paper over the endives, cover the pot, and bake in a 325° oven for 45 minutes. Remove casserole, cover, and continue to bake with the paper cover for 30 minutes more or until golden colored.   Serves 6.

You don't have to cook fancy or complicated masterpieces —
just good food from fresh ingredients.
— Julia Child

Carottes glacées — Glazed Carrots

Use fresh thyme if available, about half as much. Your best roast will be great surrounded by these beauties!

5 cups carrots, peeled, quartered,
   and cut into 2-1/2-inch lengths
1-1/2 cups brown stock or broth
2 tablespoons granulated sugar

1 tablespoon dried thyme
Salt and pepper
6 tablespoons butter

Put all ingredients into a heavy sauce pan or skillet. Bring to a boil, cover, and simmer until carrots are tender. Uncover and cook until liquid is reduced to a thick glaze.

Serves 6.

Fenouil à la grecque — Fennel Braised in Broth and Wine

This is good warm or cold and will store in the refrigerator.

6 fennel bulbs
1 cup chicken stock

1/2 cup olive oil
1 cup dry white wine

Wash, trim, and halve fennel bulbs. Put into a pot with the liquids and bring to a simmer. Cover and cook for 45 minutes or until tender. Season with salt and pepper.

Serves 6.

Crêpes de pommes de terre — Potato Pancakes

Baking potatoes are best for this; it's important to grate them at the last minute so they will not turn dark. Evaporated milk may be substituted for the cream. Chives, sage, and parsley are a good combination of herbs.

8 ounces cream cheese
3 tablespoons flour
2 eggs
Salt and pepper
1 cup grated Swiss cheese

4 cups grated raw potatoes
3 to 6 tablespoons whipping cream
4 tablespoons minced fresh herbs
2 tablespoons butter
2 tablespoons oil

In a mixing bowl, combine the cream cheese and flour; add the eggs and salt and pepper, beating until smooth. Stir in the Swiss cheese. Peel and grate potatoes. Squeeze in a towel to remove moisture. Add to mixture. Stir in cream by the spoonful until you have a thick but not runny consistency. Stir in the herbs. Heat a 10-inch skillet to moderately high heat and add the butter and oil. When the foam begins to subside, ladle in 3 portions of batter to form cakes about 3-inches wide and 1/2-inch thick. Regulate heat so that cakes are lightly browned and bubbles have appeared on the surface. In about 3 minutes, turn and brown on the other side. When done, transfer to a baking sheet and continue making cakes. Add butter and oil to skillet as needed. Reheat in a 400° oven as needed.   Serves 4.

Gratin dauphinois — Escalloped Potatoes

Potato gratins have long been a mainstay in menus all over France. Other ingredients such as anchovies, leeks, onions, and smoked ham are sometimes added. Although this can be made with raw potato slices, precooking the potatoes makes a richer tasting dish.

3 pounds baking potatoes peeled
   and cut into 1/4 inch slices
2 cups milk
3 cloves garlic, minced
3 bay leaves

Fresh ground nutmeg to taste
Salt and pepper
2 cups grated Gruyère cheese
1 cup heavy cream
Salt and pepper

Preheat oven to 375°. Put potatoes and milk in a large saucepan, adding water to cover as necessary. Add the garlic, salt, and bay leaves. Bring to a medium boil and cook until potatoes are just tender. Stir occasionally to prevent sticking. Using a slotted spoon, put half of the potatoes into a greased 9 x 13-inch baking dish. Sprinkle with nutmeg, pepper, and half the cheese and cream. Repeat with a second layer. Bake about 1 hour until golden and crispy on top.

Market potatoes and onions

Serves 6.

Chou Rouge Braisé — Braised Red Cabbage

Pork, game, or sausages are a good match for this easy dish. Chestnuts are now more readily available in the U.S.; check the Internet if you can't find them in your market.

4 strips bacon
1/2 cup thinly sliced carrots
1 cup sliced onions
6 cups red cabbage leaves cut
    into narrow slices
2 cups diced tart apples
2 cloves garlic, mashed
1 bay leaf

1/2 teaspoon ground cloves
Salt and pepper
2 cups red wine
2 cups brown stock or broth
24 peeled chestnuts
Salt and pepper
1/8 teaspoon nutmeg

On top of the stove, in a fire-proof casserole, sweat the bacon, carrots, and onions over low heat, cooking slowly for 10 minutes. Mix in cabbage leaves, cover, and continue cooking for 10 more minutes. Add remaining ingredients except for the chestnuts and bring to a simmer. Cover casserole and place in a 325° oven to continue simmering for 3 hours. Stir in the chestnuts, cover, and continue simmering until the chestnuts are tender and the liquid is absorbed by the cabbage; about 1-1/2 hours.   Serves 8.

Market cabbage and leeks

Gratin de courgettes — Zucchini Gratin

You may vary this dish by choosing your own combination of vegetables, herbs, and cheeses.

2 medium onions, thinly sliced

2 tablespoons olive oil

1-1/4 pounds ripe tomatoes, cored, and cut into 1/4-inch slices

3 small zucchini, sliced 1/4-inch thick diagonally

2 small yellow summer squash, sliced 1/4-inch thick diagonally

3 tablespoons olive oil, divided

1/4 cup fresh thyme leaves

Salt and pepper

1 cup grated Parmesan cheese

1/2 cup bread crumbs

Sauté onions in olive oil over medium heat until limp and golden; about 15 minutes. Spread in the bottom of a 2-quart baking dish. Put the tomato slices on a shallow dish; let drain. Toss squash and zucchini slices in a bowl with 1 tablespoon oil, thyme, and salt. Reserve half of the cheese and mix with the crumbs for the topping. Heat oven to 375°.

Starting at one end, lay a row of slightly overlapping tomato slices across the dish and sprinkle with a little cheese. Repeat with a row of zucchini and then a row of squash, continuing until the dish is filled. Push vegetables to compact the rows as you put them into the dish as their volume shrinks during baking. Sprinkle with salt and pepper and cheese and crumb mixture. Drizzle remaining oil over the top of all. Bake about 70 minutes or until brown and juices are reduced. Let cool at least 15 minutes before serving. May be cooked ahead and reheated. Serves 6.

Ratatouille — Eggplant Casserole

3 small eggplants, cubed
6 tablespoons olive oil, divided
5 medium onions, thinly sliced
12 stems of parsley
8 peppercorns
1 teaspoon thyme leaves
1/2 teaspoon fennel seeds

3 large sweet peppers, cored and cubed
1 bay leaf
3 medium zucchinis, cubed
3 medium tomatoes, cored and cubed
Salt and pepper
1 lemon, halved

Toss the eggplant in 2 tablespoons oil to coat. Spread on a cooking sheet and put into a 375° oven for 20 minutes.

Heat 2 tablespoons oil in a skillet. Add onions and herbs, stirring to cover with oil. Cook over medium heat, stirring occasionally, for about 20 minutes or until onions are golden. Add the peppers, stirring to mix. Continue to cook until peppers are soft.

In another skillet, heat 2 tablespoons oil over medium low heat. Add zucchini, stirring to coat and cook until soft, stirring occasionally.

Add tomatoes to the onion and pepper mixture; cook over low heat for 10 minutes.

Spoon all of the vegetables into a colander and drain juices into a pan. Put vegetables into a serving bowl. Place pan of juices over high heat to reduce until syrupy. Pour over vegetables, stirring to blend. Store in the refrigerator overnight. To serve, bring to room temperature, add salt and pepper to taste, and squeeze lemon juice over all. Serves 12.

Soufflé d'Epinards — Spinach Soufflé

A number of vegetable purées may be substituted for spinach; try broccoli, carrots, or parsnips.

1/2 cup dry bread crumbs
4 cups fresh spinach
1 teaspoon butter
1-1/2 tablespoons butter
1-1/2 tablespoons instant flour

1 cup milk
1/4 cup grated Gruyère cheese
Dash nutmeg
Salt and pepper to taste
3 egg whites

Coat 8 half-cup ramekins with non-stick spray; sprinkle in bread crumbs and place dishes on a baking sheet. Wash spinach and shake to dry. Melt butter in a sauté pan and add spinach. Cover and keep over heat for 2 minutes or until spinach has wilted. Transfer spinach to a blender, pressing out any excess moisture. Purée and put in a large bowl.

Preheat oven to 400°. In sauté pan, melt butter, stir in flour, and cook for 2 minutes or until incorporated. Whisk in milk and bring to a boil. Turn down heat and stir in cheese, nutmeg, and salt and pepper. Cool; mix with spinach.

Beat egg whites until firm peaks form. Blend 1/3 of whites into spinach mixture. Fold in remaining egg whites. Put equal portions into prepared ramekins. Reduce oven heat to 375° and bake for 20 minutes or until center is firm.

Serves 8.

Casserole aux légumes — Vegetable Medley

The vegetables may be blanched ahead of time, stored in a plastic bag, brought to room temperature, and sautéed. These crispy vegetables are good with many main dishes. Use them as needed.

4 carrots, peeled and cut into matchstick sized pieces
1 zucchini, cut into matchsticks
3 stalks celery, cut into matchsticks
1 summer squash, cut into matchsticks
2 green onions, sliced

1 sweet red pepper, cored and cut into matchsticks
1/4 pound green beans, trimmed and cut into matchsticks
1 tablespoon butter
1 tablespoon olive oil
Salt and pepper

Herbes de Provence

It is also possible to have "herbs de wherever-you-live"! Just harvest and dry the leaves from your own herb garden.

1 cup oregano leaves
1 cup thyme leaves
1 cup savory leaves
1 cup rosemary leaves
4 bay leaves

1 tablespoon peppercorns
6 sun-dried tomatoes, chopped
2 tablespoons paprika
4 cloves garlic, peeled

Dry the fresh herb leaves. Put all ingredients into a blender and pulverize. Store in a tight container for up to 1 year.

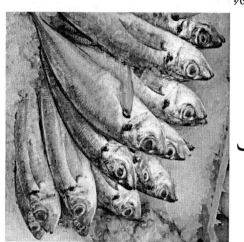

Meat, Fowl & Fish

Poulet Marie-Andrée — Marie-Andrée's Chicken

Marie-Andrée lives in the Carmargue in a beautiful chateau surrounded by fields of cattle and horses. She invited our traveling cooking class into her kitchen for instruction followed by a feast at her long dining table.

2 (4-pound) chickens, cut into pieces
Salt and pepper
1/4 cup *herbes de Provence*
4 cloves garlic, smashed
3 threads saffron

1/2 cup olive oil
1/4 cup anise or pastis
1 cup chicken broth
8 potatoes, cut into 1/2-inch slices

(continued)

Typical sidewalk menu in front of a French restaurant.

Cut each chicken into 8 pieces each; 2 legs, 2 thighs, and 2 breasts. Reserve the rest of the carcass for the stock pot. Combine remaining ingredients except the potatoes; pour over the chicken. Marinate overnight.

Dry the chicken pieces and sauté in olive oil, a few at a time. Put into a large baking pan or casserole. Bake at 325° for 20 minutes. Add the potatoes and continue baking for 20 minutes or until potatoes are tender.   Serves 8.

Poulet sauté Vallée d'Auge — Chicken as in the Auge Valley

Calvados, distilled from cider, comes from Normandy and is considered "the cook's friend." It adds a richness to cream sauces, pungency to veal and pork, and zip to fruit desserts.

1 (3-pound) chicken, cut into pieces
2 tablespoons olive oil
2 tablespoons butter
Salt and pepper
1/3 cup Calvados or applejack
1/2 cup chicken stock

2 tablespoons finely chopped onion
1/4 cup finely chopped celery
1 cup tart choppedapples
1 teaspoon thyme
2 egg yolks
1/2 cup cream

(continued)

Cut chicken into 8 pieces, saving the rest of the carcass for the stock pot. Brown the chicken in the oil and butter. Pour off almost all of the fat in the skillet, leaving chicken; season with salt and pepper.

Heat the Calvados separately; ignite the Calvados and pour it over the chicken, shaking the skillet gently until the flame dies. Add the stock to the skillet, scraping up bits in the bottom of the skillet.

In another pan, sauté the onion, celery, apples, and thyme until soft. Add to the chicken. Bring chicken to a boil, reduce to a simmer, cover, and cook for 30 minutes. Put chicken on serving platter and keep warm.

Strain remains in skillet through a sieve, pressing on solids to squeeze out the flavors. Boil the sauce to reduce to 3/4 cup. Beat egg yolks and cream together in a bowl. Slowly add pan juices; return to pan and cook over low heat for 2 or 3 minutes, stirring constantly. Pour over chicken.   Serves 4.

Poulet de Provence — Chicken as in Provence

Use fresh garlic for this dish, removing tough outer skin. Good garlic becomes almost sweet when roasted for awhile; serve this with rice to catch all the good sauce.

1 (4-pound) chicken, cut into 8 pieces
2 tablespoons olive oil
2 tablespoons butter
Salt and pepper

40 large garlic cloves
1/2 cup chicken stock or broth
1/2 cup dry white wine

Using a 12-inch skillet, brown the chicken in the butter and oil; season with salt and pepper. Set chicken aside. Reduce heat to medium and spread the garlic

(continued)

Table setting in the dining room of the Anacoluthe barge.

cloves in a layer in the skillet. Sauté about 10 minutes or until cloves are lightly browned. Return the chicken to the pan. Slowly pour in stock and wine; cover and continue cooking 20 minutes or until juices run clear when thigh is pricked. Remove chicken to serving platter. Scrape bottom of pan to loosen garlic, continue cooking to reduce sauce as needed and pour over chicken.

Serves 4.

Poulet au miel — Honey Glazed Chicken

This is a speciality of the Normandy region. Fresh quince, which are available in the fall, should be boiled gently for 10 minutes in acidulated water* before using.

1 (4-pound) chicken, cut into 8 pieces
2 tablespoons butter
2 tablespoons olive oil
2 onions, sliced
1 teaspoon sugar
1/2 teaspoon nutmeg

2 sprigs rosemary, chopped
6 to 8 quince, halved and cooked
6 apples, peeled, and quartered
1/2 cup honey
1/2 cup cider vinegar
1/2 cup chicken stock

(continued)

Brown chicken in butter and oil and set aside. Add onions and cook until golden colored. Stir in sugar, nutmeg, rosemary, fruit, and honey, mixing all together. Return chicken to skillet, turning to coat well. Cook at medium heat until caramelized. Add vinegar, scraping up pan juices. Roast in a 375° oven for 10 minutes or until juices run yellow. Remove chicken and fruit to serving dish.

On top of the stove, add chicken stock to skillet, stirring, and reducing to sauce. Pour over chicken and serve.

Serves 8.

A small amount of vinegar, lemon, or lime juice is added to water to make acidulated water. This can be used as a soak to prevent the discoloration of fruits and vegetables that darken quickly when their cut surfaces are exposed to air.

In Bresse, an area of France near Lyon, certain chickens receive the AOC designation or *appellation d'origine contrôlée*. Widely recognized for their excellence, these fowl are known by their blue feet, white feathers, and red crests. These are the colors of the French flag. In the U.S., select the juiciest, most well-fed free-range chicken you can find!

Poulet de Bourg-en-Bresse — Chicken with Cream

1 (4-pound) chicken cut into 8 pieces
2 tablespoons butter
2 tablespoons oil
1 large onion, quartered
1/2 pound mushrooms, sliced
1 tablespoon minced fresh parsley

1 tablespoon fresh minced thyme
1 bay leaf
2 cloves garlic, crushed
1-1/2 cups dry white wine
1 cup *crème fraîche*

Brown the chicken in butter and oil; add the onion, mushrooms, and seasonings. When chicken is golden, pour in the wine and allow to reduce. Add the *crème fraîche*, lower the heat to simmer, cover, and cook 30 minutes or until juices run clear.   Serves 8.

Boeuf bourguignon — Beef Stew

As boeuf bourguignon *gets better with age, this is an excellent dish to prepare ahead for company!*

1 (4-pound) blade or chuck roast, trimmed
and cut into 1-1/2-inch cubes
2 bottles red wine
3 onions, sliced
1 carrot, sliced

1/2 teaspoon thyme
1 bay leaf
1/4 teaspoon each allspice, cloves,
and nutmeg
4 tablespoons olive oil

Combine the above and marinate overnight. Before browning the meat, dry the cubes carefully. Discard marinade.

(continued)

1/2 pound bacon cut into 2-inch pieces
1-1/4 cups olive oil
1 cup flour
Salt and pepper
1 onion, sliced
1 carrot, sliced

2 cloves garlic, chopped
1/2 cup chopped parsley
1/4 cup thyme leaves
1 bay leaf
3 cups red wine
3 cups beef stock

Using a heavy ovenproof skillet, brown the bacon until crisp. Remove to the side. Add oil to the skillet as needed. Dredge the meat cubes in flour, salt and pepper, shaking excess off. Brown in the hot skillet a few at a time. Brown the vegetables. Return the bacon and meat to the pan; stir in the wine and the stock and add the seasonings. Bring to a simmer, cover, and put into a 325° oven for 3 to 4 hours.

2 tablespoons olive oil	24 to 30 pearl onions
2 tablespoons butter	1/4 cup flour
1 pound fresh mushrooms, quartered	1 cup beef stock
	1/2 cup cognac

In the olive oil and butter sauté the mushrooms, remove and set aside. Add the onions to the skillet and pour in the stock. Cook at a simmer until liquid is absorbed. Set aside.

When beef is tender, lift from pot with a slotted spoon and place in a serving bowl. Thicken the sauce by stirring in 1 cup stock combined with 1/4 cup flour. Bring to a boil and simmer 3 to 4 minutes. Stir in 1/4 cup cognac and pour over rest of the meat. Heat the mushrooms and onions and add to the serving dish.

Serves 8.

Carbonade de boeuf — Braised Beef & Onions

The beer gives a hearty taste to this stew that is especially comforting on a cold winter day.

1/2 pound bacon
6 cups sliced onions
1 (4-pound) chuck or rump roast,
   cut into 2-inch cubes
6 tablespoons butter
1/2 cup flour
2 cups beer
2 cups beef stock

2 teaspoons sugar
1 tablespoon red wine vinegar
2 teaspoons chopped garlic
1 teaspoon dry thyme
1 bay leaf
Salt and pepper
Fresh parsley

Cook bacon in a heavy skillet; set aside on paper towels. Pour off fat in skillet, reserving, and add onions to skillet. Cook over low heat until golden. Set aside onions. Heat skillet until almost smoking and add 4 or 5 beef cubes that have been dredged in flour. Brown on all sides, adding fat as needed. Put browned meat into an ovenproof casserole and continue until all cubes are browned. Add butter and stir in flour, picking up all brown bits and cook for 2 to 3 minutes or until shiny. Whisk in the beer and stock. Bring to a medium boil, whisking until the sauce thickens. Add sugar, vinegar, garlic, and seasonings, except parsley.

Add onions to the casserole and pour the sauce over all. Return to the stove and bring to a simmer. Put into 350° oven and cook for 2 hours. To serve, garnish with bacon and parsley. Serves 8.

Pot-au-feu — Boiled Beef & Vegetables

*This is rather labor intensive; you are making a favorite and celebrated feast.
A bowl of herb-flavored chick peas is a traditional accompaniment.*

2 pounds short ribs of beef
2 pounds boned beef shank
2 quarts beef stock
3 medium onions, studded with cloves
2 carrots, cut into 1/2-inch pieces
1/4 cup tomato paste

1 bay leaf
1 teaspoon dry thyme
1/4 teaspoon fennel seeds
6 peppercorns
Salt

In a soup kettle, combine meats and stock and bring to a simmer. Maintaining
the simmer, skim off foam every 15 minutes, tilting the pot to catch all the

impurities. After 45 minutes, add remaining ingredients. Continue simmering for 2 hours or until meat is tender. Remove the meat and strain the stock through a sieve, pressing on the vegetables before discarding. Wash and dry cooking pot and return the stock and the meat to the pot. Bring to a boil and add any or all of the following vegetables to the pot.

6 carrots, cut into 2-inch pieces
3 or 4 turnips, quartered

3 parsnips, cut into 2-inch chunks
6 leeks, trimmed, and cut into
   2-inch pieces

Cook uncovered over moderate heat for 30 minutes or until vegetables are tender. Prepare and cook cabbage and potatoes separately if you wish to include them in the meal.

Serves 6.

Cassoulet — French Baked Beans with Meats

There are many variations of this traditional dish, using the meats on hand at the moment. In France, goose is often part of the mix. It's important to use all the braising liquid in the final dish. You may cook the beans in the pressure cooker if speed is a factor, otherwise, I find it best to take 2 or 3 days with the different steps, assembling the cassoulet the day before serving, keeping it overnight in the refrigerator and then bringing it to room temperature before baking.

1 (4-pound) pork loin roast
3 onions, sliced
1/2 cup chopped celery

1 teaspoon chopped garlic
2 cups chopped tomatoes
1 cup wine

Put the meat in a roasting pan on a bed of the vegetables. Add wine and roast in a preheated 350° oven for 1 hour. Let cool and cut meat into 2-inch cubes. Reserve for later. Add 1 cup water to the roasting pan, stirring to scrape up juices. Reduce by half and reserve for later.

1 (3-pound) shoulder roast of lamb,
    trimmed and cubed
1/3 cup flour
3 tablespoons oil
2 onions, sliced
1/2 cup tomato paste

3 tablespoons chopped garlic
1 teaspoon thyme
1 bay leaf
2 cups dry white wine
4 cups beef stock

(continued)

Dredge meat cubes in flour and brown a few at a time in a hot skillet with the oil. Put into a roaster. Add remaining ingredients to the skillet, stirring to pick up juices, and bring to a boil. Pour over the meat, cover, and bake in a preheated 325° oven for 1-1/2 hours. Cool and reserve for later use.

5 cups great northern or navy dry beans	2 bay leaves
2 pounds ham hocks	Salt and pepper
1 tablespoon chopped garlic	Water to cover
2 onions	Bread crumbs mixed with
3 celery ribs	chopped parsley

Soak beans as directed on package. Put all ingredients together in a soup pot and simmer for 1-1/2 hours or until beans are tender but still firm. Discard the ham hocks and vegetables.

1 pound ground fresh pork
1/2 teaspoon allspice
1 teaspoon chopped garlic

1/4 cup cognac
Salt and pepper

Mix together and form into 2-inch patties. Brown over moderate heat in a skillet. Set aside.

Using a large deep baking dish, layer spoonfuls of beans and the previously roasted meat cubes alternately, ending with a layer of beans and the sausage patties. Mix all the reserved liquids with enough of the bean broth to just cover the beans. Top with a layer of bread crumbs mixed with chopped parsley leaves. Put into a preheated 375° oven. In about 20 minutes, check to see if a crust has formed. Stir it down into the pot. Turn the oven down to 350°. Stir the crust in once or twice more. Add extra bean broth if the mix looks dry. The *cassoulet* should cook for at least one hour.

Serves 12.

Caneton à l'orange — Roast Duck with Orange Sauce

This is especially good using wild duck. Rather than roasting the duck whole, we sometimes carve the breasts out of the wild ducks and use the rest for stock.

4 navel oranges
1 (5-pound) duck or 4 duck breasts
Butter
1 onion, chopped
1 celery rib, chopped
1 carrot, chopped
2 cups chicken stock

1/4 cup red wine vinegar
3 tablespoons sugar
2 tablespoons cornstarch
1 cup port wine, divided
Salt and pepper
3 tablespoons orange liqueur

Pare the orange part of the skin off the oranges and cut it into 2-inch strips. Simmer 15 minutes in water to cover. Drain and dry.

Remove the neck, wings, and any excess parts and fat from the duck. Add neck and gizzard. Chop into small pieces and brown in butter. Add 1 onion, 1 celery rib and 1 carrot, chopped. When vegetables are soft, cover all with chicken stock and simmer for 30 minutes. Drain off liquid and use to make orange sauce.

Boil vinegar and sugar until it turns into a caramel syrup. Remove from heat and stir in 1/2 cup reserved liquid. Simmer, stirring, to dissolve the caramel and then stir in remaining stock. Whisk in the cornstarch combined with the port. Add the orange strips. Simmer 3 or 4 minutes or until slightly thickened and clear. Set pan aside to be warmed later.

(continued)

Preheat oven to 425°. Pierce the duck skin all over with a kitchen fork and rub with butter. Salt and pepper the cavity and put in 1 orange, quartered. Place the bird, breast side down, on a rack in a roasting pan and roast for 30 minutes. Reduce oven to 350° and turn the bird breast side up. Continue roasting 1 hour more, or until juices run clear. Transfer the bird to the serving platter and keep warm.

Drain excess fat from the roasting pan. On high heat, add 1/2 cup port, stirring and scraping up pan juices. Reduce to 3 or 4 tablespoons. Add this reduction to the above prepared sauce and simmer, stirring for 3 to 4 minutes. Add orange liqueur and stir in remaining butter. Spoon sauce over duck and serve.   Serves 4.

Oie rôtie — Roast Goose

This is a traditional holiday meal in many parts of Europe.

1 (8 to 10-pound) goose
Salt
1 package pitted dried prunes
1 cup white wine
2 cups beef stock
1 goose liver, minced

2 tablespoons butter
2 green onions, finely sliced
1/2 cup port
1/2 teaspoon allspice
1/2 teaspoon thyme
2 cups dried bread crumbs

Prepare the bird by cutting away all loose fat, trimming the neck and cavity. Salt the cavity. Simmer the prunes in the wine and stock for 10 minutes or until tender. Drain, reserving cooking liquid. Sauté liver and onions in butter and put

(continued)

into a bowl. Put the port into the skillet and boil to pick up juices, and then add port, prunes, seasonings, and crumbs to the liver and mix together.

Lightly stuff bird with prune mixture. Prick the skin with a kitchen fork and set the bird on a rack in a roasting pan. Put into a preheated 425° oven, breast up. After 15 minutes, lower heat to 350°, turn the bird on its side, and baste with 2 to 3 tablespoons hot water. Continue turning and basting every 15 to 20 minutes for about 2 hours or until the goose is done. Test by moving and pricking a leg. If juices run yellow, it is done. Put the goose on a platter and keep warm.

Drain the fat from the roaster. Stir in the reserved wine and stock, scraping to pick up pan juices. Reduce until syrupy. Remove from heat and stir in butter. Correct seasoning and pour over goose.   Serves 8.

The basting process helps to bring the fat out of the bird. Do not overcook, or the breast meat will be dry!

Americans have a flair for casual living and a love of the informal, while the French take serious pleasure in the quality of food served and in careful presentation. Table setting with flowers and bread in baskets, left, are in the dining room of the Anacoluthe barge.

Venaison — Venison

This is a recipe from Provence. The meat is quick cooking, lean, and full flavored.

1 (3-pound) venison roast, cut into
    1/2-inch thick slices
Zest and juice of 1 orange
3 cloves of garlic, chopped
1 teaspoon chopped thyme
1 teaspoon cinnamon
1/2 teaspoon nutmeg
1/2 teaspoon pepper
1 teaspoon salt

1 egg, whipped
1 cup flour
1/2 cup nuts, chopped finely
1/2 cup olive oil
3 onions, sliced
2 teaspoons sugar
1/2 cup red wine
1/2 cup beef stock
1 tablespoon butter

Marinate venison slices overnight, using the zest, orange juice, garlic, herbs, spices, and salt.

To cook, dry meat, discarding marinade. Dip meat slices in whipped egg, then flour and nuts. Brown in olive oil; set meat aside, covered. Add onions to skillet, sauté until golden. Add sugar a little at a time, cooking over medium heat until caramelized, about 8 minutes. Return meat to skillet. Add wine and stock and bring to a simmer. Cook for 2 minutes. Put venison and onions in a serving dish; cover. Reduce liquids by half. Swirl in butter and pour over meat and onions.

Serves 4.

Lapin à la moutarde — Rabbit with Mustard Sauce

This makes a delicious meal when served with noodles and a green vegetable, such as roasted brussels sprouts. Dijon mustard, as produced in France, uses both black and white powdered mustard seeds with herbs added and mixed with verjuice. Verjuice is an acid juice extracted from large unripe grapes.

1 (3-pound) rabbit, cut into pieces
Salt and pepper
1/2 cup Dijon mustard
2 tablespoons olive oil
2 tablespoons butter

1 bottle dry white wine, divided
2 onions, chopped
1 tablespoons flour
2 teaspoons chopped fresh thyme
1 bay leaf

Myrene Hoover photo

Market scene

Salt and pepper pieces of rabbit and brush with mustard. Slowly brown in oil and butter. Remove from skillet and pour in 1/4 cup of the wine; stir to pick up pan juices. Add onions to skillet and cook until golden. Add remaining ingredients and bring to a simmer. Put the rabbit pieces into the pan, cover, and simmer for 1 hour or until meat is tender and sauce thickens. Serves 4.

Jarrets d'agneau — Braised Lamb Shanks

Roasted seasonal vegetables are an easy and tasty accompaniment to these savory morsels.

5 to 6 pounds lamb shanks
1/2 cup flour
1/4 cup olive oil
2 carrots, chopped
1 rib celery, chopped
2 tablespoons chopped fresh basil leaves
1 tablespoon chopped thyme leaves

1 tablespoon chopped garlic
2 cups chicken stock
1-1/2 cups chopped tomatoes
1 cup pitted dried prunes, cut into small pieces
2 cups red wine

Dredge the lamb in the flour and, using a heavy skillet, brown the meat in the oil. Set the meat aside and add the vegetables to the skillet. Sauté until onion is golden; add the herbs and stir in the stock, picking up pan juices. Add the shanks, tomatoes, prunes, garlic, and wine and bring to a simmer. Roast uncovered in a preheated 325° oven for 2 hours or until meat is tender. Put the shanks on a platter and keep warm.

On top of the stove, bring the sauce to a boil and reduce until thickened. Pour over the meat and serve. Serves 6.

Gigot à la moutarde — Roast Lamb with Mustard

1 (4 to 5-pound) leg of lamb
2 tablespoons soy sauce
1 tablespoon chopped garlic
1 tablespoon chopped rosemary leaves

1 tablespoon chopped thyme leaves
1/2 teaspoon ginger
2 tablespoons olive oil

Remove the thin membrane from the lamb leg. Mix the seasonings and oil together and coat the outside of the meat. Cover and marinate in refrigerator 4 hours or overnight. Roast in a 350° preheated oven 10 to 12 minutes per pound or to 145° on a meat thermometer; about 1-1/2 hours for a boned and rolled roast. Let rest 15 to 20 minutes before serving.   Serves 8.

Escalopes de veau à la crème
Medallions of Veal with Cream Sauce

Use the pink, most tender veal for this delicacy; good with rice and tiny peas.

12 medallions of veal
2 tablespoons oil
2 tablespoons butter
Salt and pepper
Juice of 1 lemon
3 tablespoons minced green onions
1/2 cup dry white wine

1/2 cup beef stock
1-1/2 cups heavy cream
1/2 pound fresh mushrooms, sliced
2 tablespoons butter
1 tablespoon oil

(continued)

Carefully flatten the pieces of veal to 1/4-inch thickness. Dry completely. Brown in sections in hot oil and butter. Season with salt and pepper and lemon juice. Set aside. Pour off all but 1 tablespoon of fat, add onions and cook for 1 minute. Add wine and stock, stirring to pick up pan juices. Reduce by half. Pour in cream and heat for 2 to 3 minutes. Add salt and pepper to taste and set aside.

In another skillet, sauté the mushrooms in oil and butter; add to cream sauce. Drain the fat. Arrange veal in skillet; season with salt and pepper and pour sauce over. Heat together for 4 to 5 minutes or until heated through; do not boil.

Serves 6.

Choucroute garnie — Sauerkraut with Sausage

4 pounds sauerkraut
1/2 pound bacon
2-1/2 cups chopped onion
4 carrots, cut into 2-inch chunks
1 teaspoon chopped garlic
1 tart apple, peeled and chopped

3 cups chicken stock
2 cups white wine or apple cider
1/4 cup gin or 10 juniper berries
Salt and pepper
6 smoked pork sausages
6 whole potatoes, peeled

Rinse the sauerkraut. Using a 4-quart stove-to-oven casserole, fry the bacon and set aside. Add onions, carrots, and garlic, and cook until soft. Stir in chopped apple and cook for 2 minutes. Stir in sauerkraut, turn heat to low, cover, and

(continued)

cook 15 minutes. Add liquids and seasoning; bring to a boil. Lay bacon on top of sauerkraut, cover and place in a 325° oven. Cook for 2 hours. Prick the sausage casing in several places and add to the casserole. Cover and cook for 30 minutes more. Boil the potatoes in a separate pan. To serve, peel the sausage and cut into 1-inch chunks. Arrange the sauerkraut on a platter and surround with sausages and potatoes.   Serves 6.

Fate cannot harm me, for I have dined well today!
                                        — Unknown

French market vendors specialize in fresh meats, as well as fish, produce, flowers, clothing, and household goods. Homemade sausages are produced on demand. The compiler of this book, Mary O. Hattery, left, is shown with a sausage maker and his wife.

Moules marinières — Mussels

4 pounds mussels
1 cup dry white wine
1 onion, chopped

4 tablespoons butter
Chopped parsley
Salt and pepper

Wash the mussels, discarding any that are partially open. Bring wine and onion to a boil, add mussels, cover, and steam over high heat for 4 to 5 minutes until all shells are open. Toss the pan occasionally to redistribute the mussels so that they will cook evenly. With a slotted spoon, lift the cooked mussels in the shells into individual serving dishes. Add butter and parsley to cooking liquid and season to taste. Pour broth over mussels. Serve with crusty bread.   Serves 4.

Poisson à la florentine — Baked Fish Stuffed with Spinach

Use salmon or snapper for this, doubling the amount of stuffing according to the size of the fish. Leave the head and tail on or remove them, as is your preference.

3 tablespoons finely chopped onion
5 tablespoons butter, divided
1/2 cup cooked spinach, squeezed dry
2-1/2 cups bread crumbs
3 tablespoons heavy cream
1/4 teaspoon lemon juice

Salt and pepper
1 (4-to 5-pound) fish, whole
1 tablespoon olive oil
1 tablespoon butter
1 cup dry white wine
1 lemon, sliced

(continued)

Jars of different kinds of honey

Sauté the onion in butter until golden; stir in the spinach. Mix in the next 4 ingredients and set aside. Prepare the fish by washing and drying well. Rub the fish inside and out with oil. In a skillet or stove-to-oven casserole, heat the oil and butter and brown the fish on both sides. Put the stuffing inside the fish. Add the wine and transfer the skillet to a 325° oven. Roast 8 minutes for each inch of thickness of the fish. Remove fish to a serving platter. Reduce juices and pour over fish. Serve with lemon slices. Serves 6.

Mousseline de poisson — Fish Mousse

This is impressive made in a fish shaped mold and served at a summer cold buffet.

6 skinned and boned fish fillets
2 cups fish stock or bottled clam juice
1 cup dry white wine
1 onion, thinly sliced
3 parsley stems and leaves
2 sprigs thyme
2 teaspoons lemon juice

1/2 pound fresh mushrooms, sliced
2 tablespoons gelatin, softened in
    4 tablespoons white wine
Salt and pepper
1 tablespoon minced tarragon leaves
2 cups heavy cream

(continued)

Simmer the fish in the next 6 ingredients for about 8 minutes or until tender. Remove fish to a blender. Strain remaining juices and return to pan. Add mushrooms and simmer 4 to 5 minutes or until tender. Remove mushrooms and set aside. Stir in softened gelatin and simmer to dissolve completely. Pour into blender with fish and pulse to purée. Pour into a bowl, stir in mushrooms and tarragon, and chill. Stir occasionally until almost set. Correct seasoning.

Whip the cream and fold into the cold fish mixture. Put into a 6-cup mold; cover and chill for several hours until set.

Unmold on a lettuce-lined platter or as individual servings on greens. Shower with chilled cooked shrimp and accompany with your best mayonnaise.

Serves 4.

Filets de poisson pochés au vin blanc
Fish Fillets Poached in White Wine

This is a classic French dish. European sole appears in the U.S. by other names; the poaching process is the distinguishing factor regarding this dish. If you have fresh fennel, you might cook the fish on a rack formed by the stems.

6 fillets of sole, flounder or other firm
   white fish
Salt and pepper
2 tablespoons butter
6 tablespoons minced onions or shallots

2 celery ribs, chopped
2 leeks, chopped
1 carrot, scraped and chopped
1 cup dry white wine

(continued)

Place half of the onions in an oiled 9 x 13-inch baking dish. Season fillets and place on top, putting the remaining onions over them. Sauté celery, leeks, and carrots in the butter for 3 minutes; put over onions. Add wine to cover ingredients. Place in a 350° oven for 8 minutes or until fish flesh flakes with a fork. Drain liquids from baking dish and reduce by half. Pour over fish and serve.

Serves 6.

The French are blessed with very good fresh catches from the sea. In many parts of the United States, we rely on frozen seafood. If you have access to freshwater fish, you will find pan frying is best. If you know a deep sea fisherman who packs his catch home, you have the best of all worlds!

Thon provençal — Tuna with Tomatoes & Herbs

4 tuna steaks
Salt and pepper
2 tablespoons olive oil
2 tablespoons lemon juice
1/2 cup minced onion

1 cup chopped tomatoes
1 tablespoon chopped garlic
3 tablespoons chopped fresh basil
3 tablespoons chopped fresh oregano

Marinate fish in oil and juice for half an hour. Sear each side of steaks for about 2 minutes per side. Set aside. Sauté vegetables and herbs in skillet for 2 minutes. Return fish to skillet and put into a preheated 325° oven. Cook up to 6 minutes or until tuna is done to your preference.   Serves 4.

We like our tuna cooked to about 1/2 inch in from the outside, and pink in the middle.

Saumon roti — Baked Salmon

This is a recipe shared by a chef on a barge on the river Seine. A rice salad, a tomato salad, and a celery root salad were served with this lunch. Crème brûlèe *completed the meal.*

1 (4 to 5-pound) salmon,
　　split lengthwise and boned
1/2 pound butter
Juice of 2 lemons

1 egg
1/4 cup water
Sea salt

Place half of the salmon, skin down on an oiled foil basket. Melt butter and whisk in lemon juice. Brush top of fillet with this sauce. Top with second half of the fish and cover all with a generous coating of egg wash. Cover with sea salt.

Using a second piece of foil the size of the first, make a butcher fold all around the salmon. Bake at 350° for 45 minutes.

To serve, remove salt and skin and top with remaining lemon butter.

Serves 6.

Montmartre *is, literally, the "Mount of Mars." It is a hill on the right bank of Paris, the center of which is the Sacré-Coeur Basilica. This area called Montmartre is also the night-life center of the city, as well as the bohemian and artistic section where many famous artists like Manet, Picasso, Toulouse-Lautrec, and Van Gogh all had their studios in the nineteenth century.*

Desserts & Other Finales

Cheese and fruit, chosen according to the season and availability locally, will often finish the main meal of the day. There are pastry shops to supply sweets when needed. But there are times when cooks wish to produce a "specialty of the house." Some of those selections follow.

Soufflé à l'orange — Orange Soufflé

As an aid to proper timing, you may fill your soufflé dish and cover it with an overturned kettle for up to an hour before baking.

2 tablespoons butter	Freshly grated peel from 1 orange
3 tablespoons sugar	7 egg whites
5 egg yolks	1/4 teaspoon cream of tartar
1/3 cup sugar	Powdered sugar
1/4 cup Grand Marnier™	

Preheat oven to 425°. Butter the sides and bottom of a 1-quart soufflé dish. Sprinkle in the sugar, tipping to cover all evenly. Set aside.

In the top of a double boiler, beat egg yolks until they are well blended. Slowly

(continued)

add the sugar as you continue beating until the yolks thicken and become pale yellow. Set over gently simmering water. Stir constantly until mixture thickens; stir in the liqueur and orange zest. Transfer to a large bowl set in a bed of ice. Stir until the mixture is cold.

Clean the beaters thoroughly. Put the egg whites and cream of tartar into a large bowl; beat until whites stand in stiff peaks when the beaters are lifted. Using a rubber spatula, fold a cup of whites into the yolks. Gently fold in the rest of the whites. Spoon this mixture into the buttered dish. Run the spatula around the top vertically about 1 inch from the outside edge so that a raised cap will form in the baking.

Bake in the middle of the oven for 2 minutes; reduce heat to 400° and continue baking another 20 to 30 minutes or until the top of the soufflé is lightly browned. Sprinkle with powdered sugar and serve immediately.   Serves 4.

Crêpes fines sucrés — Dessert Crêpes

3/4 cup milk
3/4 cup cold water
3 egg yolks
1 tablespoon sugar

3 tablespoons orange liqueur,
  brandy or rum
1-1/2 cups sifted flour
5 tablespoons melted butter
Cooking oil and butter

Put the ingredients into a blender in the order listed. Cover and blend at high speed for 1 minute. Scrape down the sides and pulse to mix. Cover and refrigerate for 2 hours or overnight.

Use a cast iron skillet or a crêpe pan; brush with equal amounts cooking oil and butter.

(continued)

Over moderately high heat, bring skillet almost to smoking. Lift from heat, pour a scant 1/4 cup batter into the skillet, rolling around to run the batter around the pan in a thin film. Return to heat for about a minute. Toss the pan to loosen the crêpe, check for light brown color and turn it over. Cook for about 1/2 minute on that side. It will be spotty; this will be the inner side. Slide off to a plate. This is your test crêpe; adjust heat, amount of batter and timing accordingly! Grease the pan, heat to smoking and proceed.

Crêpes may be kept warm under a towel or made ahead, frozen, and reheated. To serve, fill with (sweetened) fresh fruit and roll up. Top with a sweet sauce or whipped cream as you wish. Makes 10 to 12 six-inch crêpes.

Our cooking group visited a Parisian chef and his partner at their restored *mas* in southern Provence. The class was held in his spacious updated kitchen. Out the window was a conservatory greenhouse where salad greens and herbs were growing. On the opposite side of the sizable house was a wide terrace looking across a verdant kitchen garden onto a beautiful valley and far mountains. We dined at a long table seating 20. As a surprise grande finale to our meal, our hosts brought out the following dessert, *Diplomate*.

Diplomate — Molded Custard with Glacéed Fruits

Glacéed fruit is dried fruit coated with sugar. It is a specialty of southern Provence. Many markets in Provence have beautiful displays of this fruit, along with many kinds of nuts.

1 cup of diced mixed fruits
1/2 cup kirsch or dark rum
2 dozen firm, dry ladyfingers
1 envelope gelatin
1 cup milk

Zest of 1 orange
5 egg yolks
1/4 cup sugar
1-1/2 cups chilled whipping cream
1/2 cup apricot preserves

Soak the fruit in 3 tablespoons of kirsch in a small bowl. Cut a circle of waxed paper to fit the bottom of a 2-quart round mold 3 to 4 inches deep. Cut ladyfingers in half and fit them into the bottom of the pan, cut side up, in a flower petal design. Stand ladyfingers around the side, rounded side out, cutting off tops if needed. Soften the gelatin as directed on the package and keep warm.

Bring the milk and the zest just to a boil and keep warm. Beat the egg yolks, slowly adding the sugar until pale and slightly thickened. Stirring constantly, slowly add the milk to the eggs and thoroughly blend. Pour into the top of a double boiler and set over boiling water. Cook, stirring until the custard thickens and coats the spoon. Remove from heat. Blend in warm gelatin. Chill the mixture.

(continued)

Whip the cream and gently fold into the chilled custard. Fold in the fruit and kirsch mixture. Add remaining kirsch to apricot preserves; heat and stir to blend. Lightly coat the ladyfingers in the mold with the warm preserves. Ladle half of the custard mixture into the mold. Lay 3 or 4 ladyfingers across the custard and top with remaining custard. Add any remaining ladyfingers to top. Chill for 4 to 5 hours or until set. To serve, run a knife around the mold and invert on a plate, removing paper from the top.   Serves 6.

A few famous French composers:
Berlioz, Bizet, Couperin, Debussy, Fauré, Messiaen, Offenbach, Poulenc, Ravel, Saint-Saëns, and Satie

Clafoutis — Cherry Flan

Apples, pears, plums, or berries may be substituted for cherries according to the season.

3 cups pitted Bing cherries
1-1/4 cups milk
3 eggs
1 tablespoon vanilla extract

2/3 cup flour
1/8 teaspoon salt
1/3 cup powdered sugar
Powered sugar to serve

Preheat the oven to 350°. Drain cherries as necessary. Put remaining ingredients into a blender in the order listed. Cover and blend at top speed for 1 minute.

(continued)

Lightly butter a 9-inch pie plate or baking dish. Pour a 1/4-inch layer of batter into dish. Bake in oven until a film of batter has set on the bottom of the dish. Remove from oven and add cherries, and sprinkle over 1/3 cup sugar. Pour on the rest of the batter. Smooth the top of the batter with the back of a spoon. Bake in the oven for about an hour or until puffed and browned. Sprinkle with powdered sugar and serve.   Serves 6 to 8.

Myrene Hoover photo

Market fruit, Tence, France

Compote de fruits — Poached Fruit

Good combinations for compotes are Bosc pears with red wine, sugar, cinnamon, and black peppercorns; peaches with dry white wine, sugar and lemon zest. Oranges with honey and a bit of rum are tasty.

Prepare the fruit; peel and cut into desired serving size. Combine desired liquid and sweetener (see suggestions above) proportioned 2 to 1 and bring to a boil. Add fruit, keeping liquid at a simmer. Cook the fruit 5 minutes or until just beginning to soften. Remove to serving dish with a slotted spoon. Continue to simmer the liquid until thickened to a sauce consistency. Stir in desired flavoring and pour over fruit.

Crème anglaise — Custard Sauce

This custard can be dressed up with the addition of fresh seasonal fruit or fruit sauce. Comfort food at its finest!

1/2 cup granulated sugar
4 egg yolks
1-1/4 cups boiling milk

1 teaspoon cornstarch
1 tablespoon vanilla extract

In a mixing bowl, gradually beat the sugar into the egg yolks until the mixture is pale yellow and forms ribbons. Beat in the cornstarch. Still beating, gradually add the hot milk in a thin stream so the yolks are slowly warmed. Transfer to a heavy bottomed sauce pan and put over moderate heat, stirring constantly until sauce thickens enough to coat the spoon. Remove from heat, still stirring until sauce is cooled. Add vanilla extract or other desired flavoring.   Makes 2 cups.

Profiteroles — Cream Puffs

Cream puffs freeze very well. Just before serving, set them in a 425° oven for 3 to 4 minutes to thaw and crisp.

1 cup water
6 tablespoons butter, cut into
    small pieces
1 cup flour

1 teaspoon sugar
5 large eggs
1/2 teaspoon water
Crème chantilly

In a heavy saucepan, bring water and butter to boil over moderate heat. When the butter has completely melted, remove pan from heat and pour in the flour

(continued)

and sugar all at once. Beat the mixture with a wooden spoon until well blended; return to heat, stirring vigorously until the mixture forms a mass and leaves the sides of the pan. Remove from heat and make a well in the center of the paste. Crack 1 egg into well and thoroughly incorporate it into the paste. Continue to add 3 more eggs in the same manner, one at a time, beating well. The finished paste should be thick, smooth, and shiny.

Heat oven to 425°. Grease 2 baking sheets. Drop teaspoonfuls of paste onto the sheets, allowing 2 inches between. Beat the remaining egg with 1/2 teaspoon water; lightly paint this on the top of each cream puff. Bake for 6 minutes, reduce heat to 400° and bake for 5 minutes longer. Reduce heat to 325° and bake another 15 to 20 minutes or until puffs are doubled in size and lightly browned. They should be firm and crusty. Turn off the oven; make a tiny incision near the bottom of each puff to let the steam out. Let rest in the oven for a few minutes to dry out. Then remove from baking sheets to wire racks to cool.

To serve, gently slit the top of each puff and fill with *crème chantilly* (see below). Put a puddle of warm chocolate sauce on the individual serving plate, add a puff, and drizzle a little sauce over. Serves 8 to 10.

Crème chantilly is whipped cream flavored with a little powdered sugar and vanilla extract, brandy or rum. Sometimes fresh fruit is gently stirred into this, thus repeating a flavor from earlier in the meal.

Baba au rhum — Rum Cake

If you allow the dough to rise too much, it will have an over fermented yeasty taste.

1 package yeast	1/8 teaspoon salt
Water	2 eggs
4 tablespoons melted butter	2 cups flour
2 tablespoons granulated sugar	1/2 cup dark rum
	apricot jam

Soften yeast in water. Melt butter and let cool. Using a large mixing bowl, whip the yeast, sugar, and salt to make a paste. Beat in the eggs, mixing well. Stir in the flour and butter to make a sticky dough. Work the dough with your hands in the bowl; when it forms a ball, take it in your hands and pull it to a length of 10 to 12 inches, and twist. Return the dough to a ball and put it into the bottom of the bowl. Cut a cross 1 inch deep in the top; sprinkle with 1 teaspoon flour. Cover and let rise until doubled.

Butter muffin tins. Punch down the dough. Break off about a tablespoon of dough, enough to fill 1/3 of a muffin cup, and press lightly into the bottom. Continue until you have filled 12 cups. Place the tins in a warm place and allow to rise until the dough is over the rim of the cups. Bake in a 375° oven for about 15 minutes or until nicely browned. These may be frozen and warmed at a later date.

To serve, heat a syrup of 2 cups water and 1 cup sugar in the microwave until the sugar is dissolved. Stir in 1/2 cup dark rum and pour over *babas*; let soak for half an hour, basting occasionally. Drain and brush tops with apricot jam.

Serves 12.

The log and the hearth are ancient Christmas symbols reflecting warmth, nourishment, and comfort. In ancient times, it was a custom to burn a large log throughout the yule season. The ashes were then spread around the winter supply of grain and on the fields. The *bûche de Noël* cake form seems to have originated around 1870.

Bûche de Noël — Christmas Yule Log

For the cake:

3 eggs, separated
1/2 cup sugar
1 teaspoon vanilla
1/4 cup water
1 cup flour

1 teaspoon baking powder
1/4 teaspoon salt
1/4 cup cocoa
1/2 cup melted butter
Powdered sugar

Grease a 15 x10 x 1-inch jelly roll pan and line with parchment paper. Beat egg yolks until thick; add sugar gradually until you have a thick and creamy mixture. Stir in vanilla and water. Mix dry ingredients together and fold into egg mixture. Beat egg whites until they form stiff peaks. Fold whipped egg whites

(continued)

and then melted butter into batter. Spread batter evenly into prepared pan lined with parchment paper. Bake at 375° or until center springs back when pressed. Loosen cake around the edges and invert onto a clean dampened towel dusted with powdered sugar, remove parchment. Starting at short end, roll up cake and towel; cool.

For the filling:

Whip 1/2 pint whipping cream and 1 tablespoon coffee, slowly adding 1/4 cup sugar as cream begins to peak. Unroll cake carefully. Spread cream on cake and re-roll, lifting one end of toweling to start rolling. Put cake seam down on a serving plate. Cut a short piece off each end of the cake and place on sides to make tree knots. Cover all with chocolate frosting, striated to resemble bark. Add green leaves and sprinkle with almonds. Keep cool until ready to serve.

Tarte tatin is a famous specialty of the area just south of Paris. It is said to have been created at *l'hôtel Tatin* by two sisters who needed to produce a dessert quickly. The recipe following is thought to be the original, but there are many variations and different fruit may be used. Techniques vary as well, including different timing for carmelizing the fruit and whether to use the stove top or the oven. Feel free to experiment and create your own upside-down *tarte*.

Tarte tatin — Apple Pie

1/2 cup butter at room temperature	1 (1/8-inch) puff pastry sheet
2/3 cup sugar	12 inches in diameter
6 medium gala or golden delicious apples	
peeled, cored, and quartered	

Preheat oven to 350°. Spread butter evenly in a heavy 10-inch non-stick oven-proof skillet. Spread sugar as evenly as possible on sides and bottom of pan. Beginning at the edge of the pan, arrange apples in concentric circles, fitting apples closely together.

French markets feature pastry.

On top of the stove, place pan over medium heat, and cook without stirring until sugar caramelizes and turns dark golden brown; 15 to 20 minutes. Remove from heat and press gently on the apples with a wooden spoon to help fill any spaces between. Cover the apples with puff pastry, overlapping the rim of the pan. Bake until pastry is golden brown, about 30 minutes.

Remove *tarte* from oven and allow to rest for 5 minutes. Cover pan with a large plate and quickly invert *tarte;* remove pan. Serve warm.

Tarte aux pommes — Apple Tart

The pieces of tarte should be sturdy enough to eat like a slice of pizza. The method of working the dough is called "fraisage" and should result in a crisp but flaky dough.

Dough:
1-1/2 cups all purpose flour
1/2 cup instant flour
1/2 teaspoon salt
1/2 teaspoon sugar
1-1/2 sticks of butter, cubed
7 to 9 tablespoons ice water

Market apples

Combine the dry ingredients and cut in the butter to pea size. Sprinkle in water slowly, working ingredients with your fingers until dough looks crumbly and begins to hold together. Empty dough onto work surface, gathering into a 12 x 5-inch rectangle. Starting at the farthest end, moving away, use the heel of your hand to smear a small amount of dough against the surface. Continue pushing firmly away until all dough has been worked. Gather dough back into a rough rectangle and repeat process. Form dough into a ball, wrap in plastic, and refrigerate until cold and firm; about 30 minutes.

Apple filling:
4 firm apples, sliced
2 tablespoons butter, cut into
   small pieces

1/4 cup sugar
2 tablespoons apricot preserves
1 tablespoon water

(continued)

Heat oven to 400°. Peel, core, and quarter apples; cut into thin slices. Place dough on parchment paper on a baking sheet. Dust with flour and lightly roll out until dough just hangs out on all sides. Trim evenly and roll up about 1 inch of each edge to form a border. Starting in one corner, lay sliced apples in diagonal rows across dough, slightly overlapping. Dot apples with butter and sprinkle evenly with sugar. Bake until apples have caramelized; 45 to 60 minutes.

While the *tarte* is baking, mix preserves and water and heat. Strain to remove any large pieces of apricot. Brush the baked *tarte* with glaze and cool. Transfer to a cutting board and cut into serving pieces. Serves 8.

Statue of Jeanne d'Arc, Paris

In Paris, not far from the Louvre, is the famous gilded equestrian statue of Jeanne d'Arc, created by the French sculptor Emmanuel Frémiet (1824–1910) and erected in 1889. (Another version of the statue is in Philadelphia, USA.) Jeanne d'Arc was born around 1412 and died in 1431. She led the French army in a victory at Orléans that ended the English attempt to conquer France during the Hundred Years' War. After her capture by the English, she was burned at the stake, ending her brief life of nineteen remarkable years. She is the national heroine of France and was canonized as a saint in 1920.

Festivals in France

Bastille Day, *14 July each year*
This Fête Nationale, *also called* quatorze juillet *(14th of July), is celebrated throughout France and commemorates the 1789 storming of the Bastille prison in Paris, now seen as the beginning of the French Revolution. The largest celebration takes place on the Champs-Élysées, with a huge parade and large crowds.*

Tour de France, *each year, usually in July*
This world's largest cycling race was first held in 1903. Each year, the 23-day road race covers a circuit in France and neighboring countries of approximately 1,800 miles, ending on the Champs-Élysées in Paris.

Cannes Film Festival, *each year, usually in May*
One of the oldest film festivals, the Cannes Festival was founded in 1939. Located in the resort town of Cannes on the French Riviera (côte d'azur), the Festival attracts filmmakers and fans from around the world.

D-Day Invasion Anniversary, *each year near 6 June*
Although the larger observance of the 60th anniversary of D-Day is now over, each year Americans in France can take part in observance of the anniversary of this historic undertaking, the invasion of Normandy by the Allied Forces that began on 6 June 1944 during World War II. The American cemetery in Normandy at Colleville-sur-Mer is one place of commemoration.

Listing of Recipes

Salads

Alsatian Sausage & Cheese Salad · · · · · ·60
Arugula Salad · · · · · · · · · · · · ·52
Green Bean Salad · · · · · · · · · · · ·55
Gingered Fresh Fruit Salad · · · · · · · · ·59
Herb Salad · · · · · · · · · · · · · · ·50
Lentil Salad · · · · · · · · · · · · · ·53
Pears with Watercress · · · · · · · · · · ·56
Salad as in Nice · · · · · · · · · · · · ·57
Tomatoes as in Provence · · · · · · · · · · ·51

Vegetables

Artichokes· · · · · · · · · · · · · · · ·66
Asparagus · · · · · · · · · · · · · · · ·63
Braised Belgian Endive · · · · · · · · · ·76
Braised Red Cabbage · · · · · · · · · · ·84
Cauliflower with Cheese & Tomatoes · · · ·72
Dried Tomatoes· · · · · · · · · · · · · ·74

Eggplant Casserole · · · · · · · · · · · ·88
Escalloped Potatoes· · · · · · · · · · · ·82
Fennel Braised in Broth and Wine · · · · ·79
Glazed Carrots · · · · · · · · · · · · · ·78
Golden Onions · · · · · · · · · · · · · ·70
Green Beans · · · · · · · · · · · · · · ·68
Herbes de Provence · · · · · · · · · · · ·93
Peas and Lettuce · · · · · · · · · · · · ·67
Potato Pancakes · · · · · · · · · · · · ·80
Spinach Soufflé · · · · · · · · · · · · · ·90
Summer Squash · · · · · · · · · · · · · ·75
Vegetable Medley · · · · · · · · · · · · ·92
Zucchini Gratin · · · · · · · · · · · · · ·86

Meat, Fowl, & Fish

Baked Fish Stuffed with Spinach · · · · ·135
Baked Salmon · · · · · · · · · · · · · ·142

French-American Friendship

A remarkable sight along the Seine in Paris is the juxtaposition of a miniature version of the "Statue of Liberty" and the Eiffel Tower. Both structures were erected in 1889, in celebration of the centennial of the French Revolution. The 35-foot version of "Liberty" was a gift to the French from the American community in Paris, and was the original bronze model used by Frédéric Bartholdi, the sculptor of "The Statue of Liberty" that today stands in New York harbor and was a gift in 1886 to the American people from France.